If It Wasn't for the People...
THIS JOB WOULD BE FUN!

Coaching for Buy-In and Results

C.B. "Cork" Motsett, PMC

S_L^t

St. Lucie Press

Boca Raton Boston London New York Washington, D.C.

Library of Congress Cataloging-in-Publication Data

Motsett, C. B. (Charles Bourke), 1949–
    If it wasn't for the people this job would be fun! : coaching for
buy-in and results / by C.B. Motsett.
        p. cm.
    Includes bibliographical references and index.
    ISBN 1-57444-202-3 (alk. paper)
    1. Personnel management. 2. Mentoring in business. 3. Employee
motivation. I. Title.
HF5549.M674 1998
658.3—dc21
for Library of Congress   97-38461
                                                      CIP

No claim to original U.S. Government works
International Standard Book Number 1-57444-202-3
Library of Congress Card Number 97-38461
Printed in the United States of America 1 2 3 4 5 6 7 8 9 0
Printed on acid-free paper

Comments about *"If it wasn't for the people...This job would be fun! (Coaching for buy-in and results):"*

"Want to know the difference between skilled management and authentic leadership? Then don't just read this book—*study it*! Cork Motsett has packed this volume with powerful tools you can begin using immediately to revitalize your organization and increase margins. A *must read* for leaders whose agenda requires the forging of disparate competencies into the cohesion of a Special Forces "A" Team. This book is perfect for anyone who is more interested in results than theory and for anyone who is looking for a proven method of getting employees to accept responsibility for their own actions (or inactions)!"

> *Francie Dalton, President*
> *Dalton Alliances, Inc.*
> *Owings Mills, MD*

"Having worked for Cork and having used his consulting services I know his techniques work. While others pontificate about coaching, this book tells you exactly what's needed to do it."

> *Rob Goff, President and CEO*
> *Craft America*
> *Norfolk, VA*

"Who can't identify with this title? If you have ever had the responsibility of getting things done through other people, and have been frustrated by misunderstandings, miscommunications or outright hostility then this book is what you've been looking for. Read it, study it and keep it near by...you're going to be using it a lot."

Jerry Steinbrink,
Editor-in-Chief
Industrial Maintenance & Plant
Operations Magazine
Radnor, PA

"During my time of working with him, I found Cork to consistently demonstrate an uncommon leadership capability. During my association with him, I repeatedly witnessed his ability to bring divergent groups together while getting each person to accept the responsibility of doing their own jobs. This book tells how he was able to do it. It's a must read for anyone with direct supervision or management responsibility; especially if they have "difficult" people in their group!"

W.F. (Bill) Williams,
Director of Operations
Ogden Industrial Services, Inc.
New York, NY

"This book is for anyone who wants to grow from capable manager to successful leader. Cork Motsett has captured the essence of what it means to focus on results. It is for the entrepreneurial CEO who wants his or her employees to accept responsibility and expects performance from a team willing to work together to get those results. His simple five-step method makes it possible for anyone to get the buy-in needed from even the most recalcitrant employee, whether that be an hourly worker or a senior executive. This is a must read for every business owner and CEO."

Ladd M. Levis-Thorne
Chief Executive Officer
Dimensional Parking Technologies
Corporation
Boston, MA

"Cork Motsett knows what he's talking about. This book captures his proven style. This book is for anyone who wants to free up more time by getting your employees to do what they are being paid to do so you can do what you're paid to do! This book is a tremendous asset for any new manager but it's also worthwhile reading for even the most experienced executive."

Dennis Abrahamson
V.P./General Manager
RingLift
Jacksonville, FL

"As a former salesman working for Cork, I have experienced first hand his ability to lead and teach through coaching. I know of no one more qualified to write this book. The techniques and methods taught in this book are what real leadership is about. This isn't about the image of coaching, it's about getting people to accept accountability for themselves and it's about giving employees the freedom to do the job their way. This book is an extremely useful, comprehensive and tightly crafted guide that is an invaluable instrument for any manager responsible for the results of his or her people and is a tool for business executives who demand results."

Phillip Davis
Sales and Marketing Manager
PPM Incorporated
Society Hill, SC

"This book is for those who are more interested in the how than they are in the why. It's for doers and those looking for a proven method to get their employees to accept responsibility for their jobs. It's for anyone looking for a clear path to becoming an effective leader."

Richard L. Dunn
Editor
Plant Engineering Magazine
Des Plaines, IL

"With annual performance reviews becoming archaic in this age of flatter organizations, intensified project management, quick global competition and dwindling corporate loyalty, Cork hands us a new-age compass for getting things done through people. Whether our roles include responsibilities for employees, suppliers or even distributors, this book provides practical tools for binding diverse people into a common cause. He gives us an effective instrument for communicating one-on-one and focusing on results and continuous improvement, not excuses."

Jim Wilson
Dealer and Sales Development Manager
Mitsubishi Caterpillar Forklift America,
Inc.
Houston, TX

"Cork's straightforward "A-Team" analogies are good lessons for the way today's successful flat organizations operate with cross-function experience and functional expertise in a self-directed team environment. This book clearly lays out how to put egos aside as a team's expectations for success are fully understood… whether it be life or death as in military applications or in the day-to-day tides of business."

Rand McNally
Executive Vice President
and General Manager
Cleaver Brooks
Milwaukee, WI

"If you're responsible for making things happen through the actions and efforts of others under your supervision, then this book is what you need. It outlines the necessary steps that need to be taken to guarantee results. This book clearly illustrates how to develop and achieve teamwork, commitment and results."

Bill Werner
President
American Sintered Technologies,
Inc.
Emporium, PA

"The positive impact of "Coaching for buy-in and results" on the ERG Team has been immediate. There is no doubt within this organization that relying on these concepts and the workshop has been one of my best decisions to date. We have always known ERG's greatest asset, and expense, is our dedicated, loyal and capable employees. The implementation of your management tools will ensure our people strengths stays "focused on results" instead of doubling as a barrier to success."

Steven T. Jenkins
President
Environmental Recovery Group
Jacksonville, FL

"Looking back over my 45 years of management and leadership experience I can easily see that to have had the value of this handy text of solid leadership principles and proven techniques in the early stages and when I encountered "difficult" people would have been dynamite. This book deserves praise for its style and reading simplicity. Well done!"

Leonard H. Fosco
Consultant, Product Support Specialist
Plant City, FL

"This book is easy to read from start to finish and very thought provoking. It is a great asset for any manager who wants to empower his or her employees to become extraordinary performers."

Nancy Morrison, CRP
Senior Vice President
Director of Relocation
The Prudential Network Realty
Jacksonville, FL

"While the title of this book might be humorous, it presents an enlightened, straightforward approach to the age-old problem of managing people. Cork Motsett clearly illustrates and reinforces how to successfully accomplish these tasks as a coach. Reading the book I continuously thought of both current and previous members of my staff and had vivid recollections of prior situations where I could have applied the process described in this book. Any manager who applies this coaching process should see improvement in his management efforts and generate significant accomplishments in his department."

Richard Eaton, PE/CPE, CFM
CAM, CM
Manager, Facilities Engineering
Hitachi Electronic Devices (USA), Inc.
Greenville, SC
(Past President of Association for
Facilities Engineers (AFE) and AFE
Fellow)

"What a great wake-up call! After reading this book I found myself evaluating my own performance as a leader and teacher. This book provides a clear path for both the manager and employee to develop trust and understanding of both corporate and personal goals. When employees are given a chance to grow and succeed, it is a win-win situation for we are only as good as our employees."

Dennis A. Barrous
President
Essex-Silver Line Corp.
Boston, MA

"A winner by any standard! This book provides a proven leader's perspective into all of the basics of successful team building and leadership. Cork Motsett has produced a definite "Must Read" resource which should be in every successful leader's reference library."

Rear Admiral Kevin F. Delaney
U.S. Navy

"Over my 24 plus years as a supervisor, manager and executive in industry I have read many books that profess to have answers for creating results. This book gives one a no-nonsense process to create the desired results by getting employee buy-in to a common goal. Many organizations struggle today with the concept of individuals taking responsibility with delegated authority. This book ties the two together into their logical relationship. As the "new empowered teams" are formed in companies victimized by downsizing and reengineering, the principles in this book are a must to create an atmosphere of acceptance and buy-in from ALL employees, not just the boss. This common-sense approach outlines the necessary path to creating the performance-based team within each of our organizations."

John L. Blumenshine. PE/CPE
Vice President
S&C Electric Company
Chicago, IL

"People can really make the difference in your business. Knowing how to find and recruit the right people for the job is critical. Now what?! Equally important is employee development and motivation. This takes strong leadership "know how." Cork Motsett's book teaches us how to lead our employees more effectively.

I am excited about using this book as a client gift. It is very valuable information that any executive, manager, supervisor or parent will appreciate."

Sally K. Bales
Founder & President
The Bales-Waugh Group
First Interview, Founder &
Vice President
SearchNet International, Founder &
Vice President
Jacksonville, FL

"Without question this book cuts through the fluff and gets right to the point. The information presented is "right on the money" and an invaluable tool in how to lead for results, (notice I didn't say manage!) in today's business world.

This book is an important piece in my reference library!"

Jim Howick
President
Physicians Online
Jacksonville, FL

"A valuable spin on our premise that excuses are the root of all evil in the workplace."

Dr. David G. Mutchler
James M. Bleech
Co-Authors
<u>*Let's get results, not excuses!*</u>
Grand Rapids, MI

About the Author

C.B. "Cork" Motsett is the founder and President and CEO of Business Development Specialists, Inc., an "outcome-based" sales and marketing consulting company. He is a recognized leader in sales, marketing and leadership development with more than 22 years of strategic and tactical success with both Fortune 500 and entrepreneurial start-up companies. He has a well-earned reputation for consistently delivering results on both a national and international basis, having worked and lived throughout the U.S., Mexico, Canada, the Pacific Rim, Europe and the Caribbean. He has authored numerous published articles and is a repeat presenter and seminar leader at national, international and regional conferences. His greatest strength is his ability to develop strong, effective leaders and performers who generate long-term results.

His leadership skills were recognized and honed at an early age. He entered the U.S. Army out of high school and rose to the rank of Sergeant E-5 before accepting a commission as a 2nd Lieutenant just 12 days after his 20th birthday. He was one of the youngest officers to command a U.S. Army Special Forces "A" Team. During his second tour in Vietnam, he was selected to become a member of the Special Operations Group, an elite group within Special Forces that ran clandestine operations in Northern Laos and North Vietnam. It was at this time that he became one of the few who successfully escaped after being held as a POW.

Mr. Motsett is an accredited Professional Management Consultant (PMC). His is also a past Chairman of The Executive Committee (TEC) and has, since 1986, been repeatedly selected for inclusion in *Who's Who in Finance and Industry* and has also been repeatedly included in *Who's Who in Emerging Leaders, Who's Who in World Leaders* and *Who's Who in America*. He was most recently selected to the Editorial Review Board for *Industrial Maintenance and Plant Operations Magazine* and provides editorial review for *Plant Engineering* Magazine. A graduate of the University of South Florida, he and his family live in Jacksonville, Florida.

Acknowledgments

My thanks go to Ms. Mimi Williams, who performed the task of editing this book, for her phenomenal patience during the multiple correction and revision sessions and for her help and suggestions.

A thanks also goes to Ms. Francie Dalton, President of Dalton Alliances, who provided much needed encouragement and support; especially during the initial concept stage when I needed it most.

I also want to recognize and thank Jim Bleech and David Mutchler of Leadership Development Corporation and co-authors of *Let's get results, not excuses,* 1994, published by MBP Press, Grand Rapids, MI. Jim and David identified and developed many of the concepts included in Chapter III, Creating a "No Excuses" Culture. I strongly believe that the concepts developed by Jim and David are absolutely essential to effective coaching.

Additional thanks goes to J. Charles Plumb who has graciously allowed me to adopt his term, "Parachute Packers" and to incorporate it in step 4 of the coaching process (detailed in Chapter VIII). Charlie is one of the very best motivational speakers and his message of Courage, Choices and Commitments: *Making Tough Choices in Challenging Times* should be heard by every leader and employee who is interested in developing a better team.

Finally, I want to recognize and thank the literally hundreds of managers, professional writers and consultants who have influenced my thoughts, beliefs and philosophy on coaching, motivating and empowering employees over the years. I also want to single out *The Harvard Business Review* and *Sales & Marketing Management* magazines as fantastic sources for informative and thought-provoking articles on the subject of leadership and motivation. If I have inadvertently included thoughts or concepts without giving proper credit or attribution I offer my sincerest apologies.

Dedication

I want to dedicate this book to my wife Mary who has stood by me for more than 24 years in good times and bad; who has been with me during our moves and my travels throughout the United States and across the globe to Latin America, Mexico, The Caribbean, Canada, The Pacific Rim and Europe; who has always been there when I needed her, and who has always been my best supporter and my best friend.

I also want to dedicate this book to my three children, Jon, Jill and Brian, who have been my greatest challenge and greatest joy. Each has challenged me to be consistent and to be honest. Each has been a willing participant in this coaching process.

Finally, I want to dedicate this book to:

Captain Doug Gray, United States Army, Infantry, 5th Special Forces Group (Airborne), killed in 1969 in Pleiku Province, Republic of South Vietnam, who taught me the "process" of coaching.

Sergeant First Class (SFC) Michael Brown, 5th Special Forces Group (Airborne), Special Operations Group (SOG), killed in 1970 in Northern Laos, who taught me the meaning of true leadership.

Table of Contents

Introduction

> *The role of the CEO (sic. Leader): "be a great coach, be a great talent scout, and ask the right questions."*
>
> *John Zeapfel*

Why is it that some employees only do exactly what you tell them to do, when you tell them to do it, while others look for opportunities to contribute even more than is expected? How is it possible to tell someone exactly what you need done and have them acknowledge they understand only to find an hour, or a day, later that they claim not to have understood what you wanted?

If it wasn't for the people...this job would be fun (Coaching for buy-in and results) provides executives, managers and supervisors the techniques needed to ensure employees *willingly* and *consistently* perform to ever higher levels of expectation. This book offers a simple, but highly effective, five-step formula that

1

guarantees successful empowerment. More importantly, this process effectively transfers the responsibility for an employee's actions, or inactions, squarely onto the employee's shoulders... where it belongs.

Over the last few years much has been written about the importance of empowerment and coaching but precious little has been written about "how" to empower and coach subordinates. This book provides the process in an easy to understand and follow five-step process that can be used by leaders at every level of an organization.

Here is the proven process that has turned "maliciously obedient" employees into positive, contributing team members. After reading this book and applying this five-step process, you will know how to effectively coach even the most recalcitrant employee and have the techniques to ensure continued development.

The Origin of the Process

My first experience implementing "Coaching and buy-in" came when I was 20 years old and just recently commissioned as a Second Lieutenant. I had just completed the Special Forces' qualification and training program and was given command of a Special Forces "A" Team at Fort Bragg, North Carolina with the 7th Special Forces Group. Typically, a Captain with at least three to four years of command experience commands an "A" Team. However, because of the war in Vietnam, there was a shortage of qualified officers.

Faced with command of a highly specialized unit consisting of 10 mid-level and senior Non-Commissioned Officers ranging in rank from Staff Sergeant (E-6) to Master Sergeant (E-8), all with eight to 15 years of experience in their specialties, I learned the most important lesson of my life. I learned that command doesn't mean doing the other person's job for them. I also learned that even though each member of the team was older, had far more experience and was better qualified in his own specialty, I could get the best results *not by telling these experts "how" to do their jobs* but by making sure they knew and understood what was expected of them. And then *allowing them to do their jobs as they knew best.*

What saved me from making a fool of myself and failing at my first command was the help and support of a good friend, Captain Doug Gray, a West Point graduate whom I had met during Special Forces training. Immediately after the change of command ceremony, Doug invited me into his office and asked me just how I intended to run this team as such a raw,

3

young officer. How, he challenged, was I going to gain the acceptance of the team, influence its action and be responsible for its success? In essence, how was I going to gain the acceptance of a group of highly trained and experienced professionals, and how was I going to keep from losing control and fulfill my responsibility as team commander.

After stuttering and stammering "Truisms" it became obvious to me that I had no concrete ideas about the specifics of how I would handle this important responsibility. Doug, who had already commanded at company level and who had plenty of experience in troop command, shared with me his method of success. He offered a very simple process that, when followed, would ensure strong, two-way communication between the members of the team and myself. Doug taught me a process that puts the responsibility of action squarely on the shoulders of those who are supposed to carry it out.

Using the process he taught me, I was able to quickly gain the acceptance of my more experienced Non-Commissioned Officers. As I followed Doug's technique, I was able to ensure that everyone understood what their responsibilities were (including me), what was expected of them and, most importantly, that they assumed responsibility for their own actions and the results of those actions. In what is truly a "No Excuses" environment, I learned that coaching and command go hand-in-hand to form true leadership ability.

Tested by combat in Vietnam and a management career of more than 22 years, I have used this same concept over the years and it has worked every time. Over time this simple process has evolved to become the full-blown process presented in this book, but its foundation remains basically unchanged after all these years.

Chapter I

A Simple Process of Leadership

> *"Make people believe what they think and do is important and then get out of the way while they do it."*
> *Jack Welch*

Over the years I have learned much from the managers and executives I've worked for as well as from my peers and support staff. During my years of Active and Reserve Military Duty and my formal management experience, I've been fortunate to work with, and learn from, some of the best leaders, managers, trainers and consultants in the industry. All these experiences have been applied to formalize my thoughts and beliefs into a leadership philosophy and understanding that is incorporated into five distinct steps. The core of this concept, though, is based on two overriding assumptions.

7

The first assumption (which is more of a philosophical concept) is that a leader is responsible for clearly identifying the goals and vision he or she wants the team to pursue. Fundamental to this belief is that it is the leader's sole responsibility to ensure everyone on the team is focused on obtaining the results envisioned in the goal. Equally important, it is the leader's responsibility to ensure that the team's energy and efforts are focused on obtaining results; not finger pointing or fault finding. (This is the essence of the "No Excuses" Culture described in Chapter III.)

The second assumption is that the leader's subordinates, (employees) are technically competent and are adequately trained to do their jobs. If this is not true, then no amount of coaching or empowerment will succeed in reaching the goals of the organization.

If these assumptions are correct and your employees have the technical competence to do their jobs, then the leader must demonstrate respect and confidence in his or her subordinates by allowing them to determine the best way to do their jobs within the established confines and parameters. This simple philosophy of leadership made it possible for a 20-year-old "raw" officer to successfully lead an Army Special Forces "A" Team. The evolution of the coaching process and its consistent application have allowed me to grow into successive corporate leadership positions and have been the basis of my ability to effectively develop outstanding employees.

As a sales manager and executive, I've had the opportunity to manage sales forces of as few as five people to nearly 200 with intermediate levels of management support. I've worked with sales forces consisting of in-house sales representatives, independent manufacturers' representatives and combinations of the two.

What I've found to be the key to leading highly charged sales forces is that sales people need to become empowered -- to be led not managed. More than anything else, this undeniable tenet has been the conduit for turning what Jim Bleech, co-author of *Let's get results, not excuses*, calls "coffee house cripples" into star performers.

True leadership success is the ability to turn ordinary people into extraordinary performers. This process gives the leader the tools for successful leadership and the ability to let ordinary people become extraordinary performers. Well-trained, competent and motivated people -- just like Special Forces troopers -- can't be told *(very effectively)* how to do their jobs. You've got to make sure they know what is expected of them, what the objective is, and what the parameters are; then get out of their way!

9

What you have to do is to give your employees a clear understanding of what you consider to be acceptable results and a clear definition of the difference between success and failure. As the coach, your job is to make sure your team understands what the goals are and what you want them to accomplish. Your job as the coach is to set parameters to include the standards of acceptable and unacceptable behavior, time lines and work ethics.

The end result, once you have the job parameters in place and a clear understanding with your employee of the goal, is to loosen the reins and let them do it their way. By giving employees the ability to use their own creativity and then holding them accountable for their results, you unleash their creative powers and turn ordinary employees into extraordinary producers.

I've worked with sales representatives who are excellent verbal presenters and some who are terrible; some who are true extroverts and some who are truly introverts, who are very quiet and very shy. Strong, positive sales executives don't fit a single mold. They all make do with their own talents, their own strengths and their own personalities.

With all the personality styles that exist in today's workforce, especially an international workforce, it's not possible to have one type of sales person. The key for the leader is to give each person the tools and the understanding he or she needs to achieve the end result.

Coaching for Buy-In and Results Works in Every Department.

This process is not limited to just sales people. It works with virtually every employee level from the lowest, minimum-wage position to the most top-level, senior executives.

As vice president and general manager of a division of a multi-billion dollar service company, I had the responsibility to manage a work force of over 1,000 employees and annual sales approaching $50 million. I was again in a situation very similar to my Special Forces experience: I had the responsibility of supervising and managing employees with many years of experience in their specialties, who knew much more than I did about the specifics of doing their jobs.

Since I didn't know how to do what they did I didn't try to do their job for them. I achieved the division's objective by coaching each of these individuals. Each was given a clear vision of the goal, an understanding of the standards of acceptable and unacceptable performance, and the understanding that

11

it was their job to perform to the very best of their ability to achieve the end result. As the coach, my job was to ensure they understood what was expected of them, to provide the support they needed and to coordinate their activities with the rest of the team.

Why the Process Works

The key to successful coaching is buy-in and acceptance of responsibility. The coaching process provides the road map to get to this point. It makes no difference what professional level you're working with. I've experienced coaching people in a variety of roles, from technicians and engineering professionals to administrative and support personnel; from hourly laborers to skilled craftsmen; and from newly hired sales representatives to highly experienced and skilled sales and marketing professionals: the process works. (It also worked with my children, especially during their teen years.)

On a Special Forces team, the team commander is not expected to be the demolition expert, the weapons expert, logistics expert, medical expert or communications expert. His expertise is to bring them all together and get them marching in the same direction with a clear understanding of the goals and objectives and how their specific expertise is to be applied. It's no different in industry and commerce.

The leader has to lead and let his or her employees do the job to the best of their abilities.

This process, perfected over the years, has enabled me to create a very strong team with a positive morale, by making people accountable for their own actions and responsible for the results of those actions. This, in turn, gives them the sense of pride and accomplishment that comes with taking ownership of a job well done.

Whether managing as sales manager, as an executive with responsibility over sales and marketing, as a general manager over an entire division or department, or as the president and CEO, the requirements and techniques are the same. You must demonstrate the ability to efficiently and effectively communicate with your employees; create a common vision of company goals; provide an understanding of the employee's role in getting the job done; ensure the employee has an understanding of what is expected of him and, what are considered acceptable and unacceptable results.

As Steven Covey says in his book *The 7 Habits of Highly Effective People,* start with the end in mind. The very first step of this process is the buy-in of the end result, the goal. Once you have the buy-in, the rest of it seems to fall into place.

Buy-in allows for the effective development of a working relationship even with what historically are opposing sides. Using this process, you can bring people together to form a team. For example, I have used this process when working with union leaders on several occasions both in start-up and during the job. Responsible for the actual negotiations, I found this technique effective in this situation, too. What I attempted to do, and what I was successful in doing, was achieving a "buy-in" with the unions -- the understanding that we shared a common goal, a common mission.

Starting with the end in mind, we reached agreement on the importance of satisfying the client's needs to complete the job within budget and on schedule. By focusing on what's in it for them, the union, we were able to reach a common ground and a mutually agreed upon objective. Once the buy-in was in place regarding the common objective, we could work together instead of against each other.

While not a formal part of the coaching process, it is critical to understand the importance of accepting the responsibility of leadership. The entire coaching process is built on the foundation of leadership and the premise that the coach will accept the responsibility of being a leader. This philosophical understanding of the role and responsibility of a leader is fundamental to effective coaching. To state it simply, if you are not willing to accept the role and responsibilities of leadership you cannot become an effective coach. At the most basic level it has to be understood that only leaders can be coaches.

And this means, that as the leader, you have to accept responsibility for clearly communicating the goals. Most importantly though, as the leader you must accept the responsibility for ensuring communication exists between you and your subordinates. You can't assume they know what you want accomplished; you have to take responsibility for ensuring that they know what the objective is; what you expect from them. Simply stated, if there's a failure in communications, it's your failure. It also means that, as the leader, you ensure the team, including yourself, is focused on results; not finger pointing or fault finding. This is what accepting the responsibility of leadership means.

In the end, the ability to become an effective coach is dependent on your ability to become an effective leader. As you will realize as you progress through the following chapters, most of the important changes that will occur will not be so much changes you effect in others but changes in you and how you relate with others in your organization. The essence of leadership is not so much to manage and change others as it is to manage and change yourself.

Chapter Summary

Key points in this chapter included:

- Effective coaching can only be done by a leader.

- Leaders manage people -- managers manage things.

- Leaders identify and communicate the goals -- they keep everyone focused on the vision of success and what it takes to be successful.

- Leaders let their people do their work within the established parameters and guidelines.

- It is the leader's responsibility to determine if his or her employees are adequately trained and competent in their job positions. If an employee is not technically competent to perform his or her job function then they must be trained <u>before</u> the coaching process can work.

- The key to effective buy-in and coaching is empowering employees to accept the responsibility for their actions, or inactions.

Notes

Chapter II

What's Changed Over The Years?

"The first step on the road to decline is failure to listen"

Ralph Shaw

It has long been recognized that the single biggest problem most executives, managers and supervisors face is working through other people. This problem is further exacerbated when subordinates take on an attitude of indifference or outright hostility. The fantasy is that in years past managers could just force their will on the problem maker or, if that did not work, they could simply fire him and be done with it. The reality, however, is that this was rarely the case.

Managers, particularly executives, have rarely

19

had the luxury to hire and fire at will. There have usually been extenuating circumstances that prevented the arbitrary firing of employees except at the lowest levels of unskilled labor. Sometimes it was the unique skills or talents the person held, sometimes it was the lack of readily available replacements, and sometimes it was the rush of the moment, "political" considerations or something else.

The situation today isn't much different. However, in some ways it's much harder for a manager to fire, or even discipline an employee. With continued downsizing/right sizing, departmental reengineering, budget cuts and restricted growth, increasing equipment sophistication and increased need for technical training and experience, it is getting much more difficult to find qualified people and even harder to train replacements. Add to this recent government regulations and case law impacting "employee rights," and we see even more clearly the need to better manage and motivate employees; i.e., the vital importance of coaching.

This is further complicated when you add in many employees' feelings of insecurity caused by downsizing and increasing competitive pressures. This is addressed later in this chapter, but leaders have to be aware of it as they begin using the coaching techniques described in this book.

The truth is that we have no other choice but to get better results from our employees. Careers are dependent on our ability to maximize the results we are able to realize from our people. Our people skills, particularly our ability to motivate and lead, are now the single most important skill senior management looks for when determining career advancement potential.

One of the critical points Doug Gray taught me when he first explained his coaching/leadership process was to have respect for the technical competence of the NCOs (Non-Commissioned Officers)—my employees and the importance of consistently demonstrating my confidence in their abilities. Recognizing their professionalism required that I let them determine the best way to do their job within the parameters I established.

Managers Must Be leaders

The days of the dictator -- of telling people what to do and how to do it -- are long gone. One of the significant results of corporate downsizing and re-engineering is the elimination of most middle-management positions. This means executives, managers and supervisors all have more people reporting directly to them. IBM's rule of seven, that no manager or executive could effectively manage and

21

control more than seven direct reporting subordinates, is a management maximum that died with the recessions of the late '70s and '80s. Additionally, increased international competition has resulted in the organizational reengineering and downsizing that has swept through almost every business these past two decades.

Today, it is far more common to see supervisors, managers and executives leading teams of 10 to 15, and sometimes even more than 20, employees as organizations stretch themselves to become flatter, more responsive and less costly.

As a result, we have less time to oversee and inspect what our employees do. We have no choice but to ensure the successful empowerment of our employees so that the work will get done. The alternative is totally unacceptable...a noticeable reduction in production and productivity as our employees stand around waiting for us to authorize what they are capable of doing themselves.

Listening Is Still Fundamental

The need to listen to our employees isn't new...it goes as far back as management and employee relations have been studied. An article in the September-October 1957 edition of *Harvard Business*

Review cited a study which identified that the No. 1 employee complaint was that their bosses didn't listen to them: "many employees felt they weren't listened to...that they weren't part of the team." The focus involved a survey of top executives of a major manufacturing plant in Chicago who were surprised to discover just how important (*and difficult*) listening was to accomplishing the team objective. If it was a problem then, it's even more so today.

Effective Coaching Requires Disciplined Listening

Most employees want to contribute but they have to be given the opportunity. Nearly 40 years after the article appeared in the *Harvard Business Review*, employees still have, at the top of their list of biggest complaints: "management won't listen to us." After an exhaustive search for solutions to this problem one thing becomes clear: The managers who are carefully listening to the concerns of their top performers are the ones who have the best chance of getting the maximum commitment and productivity from them. These managers also have the best chance of keeping them on board when job security can no longer be guaranteed.

Again, this is not new. In another study published in the January-February 1969 issue of

Harvard Business Review, Paul R. Lawrence, in his article: "How to deal with resistance to change," cited specific case study examples of increased employee cooperation, productivity and acceptance of change. In each situation where positive results were obtained the key factor was the leader's willingness to listen to the employee and, where appropriate, incorporate their suggestions. The single element that determined success or failure was the leader's -- manager's, willingness to listen and the employee's understanding that he was contributing to the solution. Even in those instances where the employee's specific suggestions were rejected, there was measurable and observable improvement as long as the leader actually listened to the employee.

This study is nearly 30 years old and there have been numerous studies citing similar findings and results. So why do most employees rate managers and leaders who actively listen to and solicit input from their employees the exception rather than the norm?

- Could it be that only a few companies invested the time and effort to effectively train and develop those skills in newly appointed managers and leaders?

- Could it be that we simply expect newly appointed managers to just "intuitively know" what to do and how to do it?

- Or could it be that we just haven't recognized the importance of disciplined listening.

The bottom line is that effective coaching requires disciplined listening.

The Key To Success Is Still A "Win-Win" Relationship

Managers have to listen to effectively lead. Hand-in-hand with this fundamental leadership technique is the realization that we no longer manage groups -- we manage individuals! A classic example of the problems incurred from not listening is this "shocking" scenario as reported in "Mind Reading" by Geoffrey Brewer *(Sales & Marketing Management,* May 1994):

> To the surprise of his sales manager and colleagues, a top performer made an ugly gesture and stormed out of a black-tie dinner party. The reason? After a request *not* to receive yet another plaque for his contribution as Salesman of the Year, he was presented with -- what else -- a plaque.

Finding out what drives your top performers, be it pride, happiness, money, or something else, is your competitive edge in a highly competitive marketplace.

What this means is that part of managing individuals is learning to understand what motivates and drives the individual members of your team. The importance of this point will be self-evident when you master Step 2 of the Coaching Process—Tell 'em "Why"...Not "How."

Money Is No Longer The Prime Motivator

It's clear communication and involvement that motivate. But each person is different. Just as you can no longer manage groups, you can't motivate groups either... motivation is a one-on-one exercise. Social scientist Frederick Herzberg identified six motivators of employees. In stark contrast to the unflattering notion that money is the prime motivation for all employees, Herzberg noted these six prime motivators:

1)   Achievement
2)   Recognition of achievement
3)   The work itself
4)   Responsibility
5)   Advancement
6)   The possibility for growth

As Herzberg points out and what I've found to be true in case after case, is that people want to grow and advance in their careers. Employees will be unhappy, and therefore under-utilized, if they're stuck doing the same kind of thing year after year, especially if they're not given the opportunity to improve their skills and do their job better. This does not necessarily mean promotion to supervision or management. In fact, it is only a small percentage of employees who actively look for the specific responsibilities and challenges associated with supervision and management; especially if it only represents 50 cents an hour difference in pay or forsaking overtime pay. What is being referred to here is an employee's desire to be challenged by the responsibilities of the job itself and the opportunity to take on more important tasks and become more effective at what they do.

Today's employees, now more than ever, want to be treated as adults. Most employees want to be made to feel part of the team, not just a cog. The entrepreneurial spirit of top performers is sometimes squashed by mere monetary reward. At the very core, employees want ownership of what they do. Providing ownership is the cornerstone of allowing employees to accept responsibility for their actions and paramount to a leader's ability to impact behavior changes. As Maurice Mascarenhas has so effectively stated it:

"A feeling of ownership changes behavior -- no one ever spent a summer afternoon washing a rental car."

Entrepreneurs fuel their careers and the careers of those around them with intrinsic rewards -- the positive outcomes that result from an activity itself rather than from what is ultimately obtained from engaging in the activity, i.e., only financial rewards. By sharing ownership and the challenges and rewards associated with being part of the team, leaders strike at the very heart of ownership and motivate employees to accept responsibility for both the successes and failures of the team. They also allow their subordinates to grow professionally; to realize their best potential.

Again, I return to my experience in Special Forces, no one volunteers -- for the money alone -- for this type of difficult training and qualification or the dangerous missions. They do it for the challenge and satisfaction of being the "best of the best." By the way, the only monetary reward associated with undertaking the strenuous challenge of becoming qualified to wear the beret is associated with being on jump status. (When I was on active duty this was a mere $55 a month for enlisted men and $110 a month for officers.)

It's the same in business. Entrepreneurs risk everything they have to create a business, to bring a

28

new product or service into existence. While there is the chance of financial reward, it's not just the money that motivates, but, more often than not, it's the challenge.

In my own case, I left a multibillion dollar company where I enjoyed a six-figure income and the benefits and security of an established company and position to join a start-up company that offered the opportunity and challenge of bringing a totally new product to life. I didn't leave the security of a high paying position for more money... I left for the challenge. And I know that I'm not unique. Ask any experienced headhunter to identify his most effective recruiting technique and he will almost always respond that it is his ability to capture the challenge and opportunity of the position for which he is recruiting.

Why should we think differently of our employees? Coaching for buy-in and results allows you, as the leader and coach, to motivate your employees with something far more valuable than money. You can motivate them with the sense of achievement, recognition of achievement, the work itself, responsibility, advancement, and the possibility for growth.

Building Employee Loyalty

Today's employees are mad as hell and they're not going to take it anymore! The days of job security and pensions, by and large, are behind us. The challenge for leaders is to find ways to maintain and increase company loyalty and commitment to ever increasing performance standards. There are several ways of doing it, but to effectively implement any of these strategies requires clear, two-way communication and the ability to achieve employee buy-in and commitment. It takes effective coaching to inspire loyalty, hard work and creativity. But more than anything else it requires leaders who are willing to empower their employees.

But what is empowerment? It's an often-used term that tends to mean different things to different people. For the purpose of this book and the coaching process, I will use the following formula to serve as the operating definition:

$$\boxed{E = R \times A \times C}$$

where   **E** = Empowerment
         R = Responsibility
         A = Authority
         C = Coaching

30

What this definition clearly states is that empowerment cannot exist if any of these components on the right side of the formula are missing. The rules of math dictate that anything multiplied by zero results in zero; this is the reason each component is multiplied instead of added.

The empowerment formula requires the employees to accept responsibility (**R**) for their own actions or inactions; for performing their job within an acceptable level.

It also requires the leader to give the appropriate amount of authority (**A**) necessary to do the work to the employee. If the employee has to ask permission before taking action in his assigned area of responsibility, then it's nearly certain that the employee is **not** empowered. There are obviously areas such as quality and safety where variations to established policies and procedures must be reviewed and approved prior to making changes. But, except for these obvious exceptions, the employee must be free to determine the best way to do his or her job... free of the necessity for "asking for permission" before taking action.

The final element of this formula is active coaching (**C**) by the leader. This is how the employee keeps the leader informed and how the leader effects change. When it exists, effective empowerment is a critical factor in creating employee loyalty to both the management team and the company; but it is not the only factor.

Robert Swain, a New York-based management consultant, is quoted by Geoffrey Brewer in "Seven Secrets to Building Employee Loyalty When You Can't Promise Job Security," *(Sales and Marketing Management, December* 1995*)*:

"The most enlightened companies are being honest. They're telling their people that because of competitive pressures, they can't guarantee security. But they can find ways to challenge employees, help them grow and develop, and reward them so that they'll at least have a sense of excitement and self-esteem about their work."

Brewer's seven secrets to building employee loyalty and commitment follow the comprehensive coaching process I've outlined, building upward from a strong foundation:

> 1. *Set High Expectations*
> "Highly motivated people love to over-come challenges. And they'll stay with companies that continually set demanding goals," writes Brewer, who illustrates his point with a look at Stryker Corporation's 'no excuses' work

32

environment. Management executives at this medical equipment company in Kalamazoo, Michigan, set an expectation for each of its division's profits to grow by 20 percent every year. Company officials are quoted as saying that, "winners love this environment." Stryker has achieved its 20 percent increase in each division for the past 18 years.

2. ***Communicate Constantly***
Brewer writes, "Employees are fed up with being kept in the dark, or lied to, by management. Nothing demoralizes a work force more than hearing one day how bright the future looks, and the next day reading in the paper that the company may be merging or selling off operations." Stuart R. Levine, CEO of Dale Carnegie & Associates, Inc., a training company in Garden City, New York, stresses two-way communication both formally in the form of videos distributed to company offices world-wide, and informally with eye contact and listening skills. "You can instill a lot of trust in people just by looking in their eyes and listening," Levine said.

3.   ***Empower, Empower, Empower***
At Hewlett-Packard, Brewer quotes Mike
Borg, United States marketing manager
for desktop PCs for Hewlett-Packard in
Palo Alto: "We rely on people who are
closest to day-to-day activities to make
decisions, with support and some guid-
ance from management. People know
they can make their ideas come to life
here, they can make a difference, and
that's the best opportunity we can offer
them."

4.   ***Invest in Their Financial Security***
"If job security is dead, so   too is that
relic of Corporate America's fatter years:
the company pension. Most people who
don't know the difference between a
money market account and a mutual fund
are now forced to finance their own
retirements. They need help -- and
money -- now," Brewer writes. He
quotes Arnie Weimerskirch, vice president of corporate quality for Honeywell:
"The strategy here is to promote
ownership of Honeywell stock by all
employees. When you're an actual owner
of the company, instead of a theoretical
owner, you have a real stake in the
company and its future."

According to Levine, it's all about boosting employee self-esteem. "If you have your finances in order, just as if you're well-trained or recognized for your accomplishments, you develop a strong sense of self-esteem. People get this feeling when you show that you care about them. They want to see it in dollars and cents and they want to see it in intangible ways. They'll stay with you and work hard for you, just as long as they see that you care."

5. *Recognize People as Often as Possible*
Building a sense of camaraderie and trust in a workplace that no longer offers security includes recognizing your employees in every way, and as often as possible. Dale Carnegie, through Levine, began a program called "I Caught You Doing Something Right." Every week an employee receives a $250 cash reward for a job well done. Employees nominate each other, promoting the successes of their colleagues and friends.

"Giving out a paycheck helps people pay the bills, but it doesn't buy loyalty. Being rewarded for accomplishments is a vital part of any individual's needs. These

35

awards keep people excited about being here," Brewer quotes Weirmerskirch as saying.

6.   ***Counsel People on Their Careers***
Career growth has become a challenging maze of lateral moves. Debra Sieckman, director of sales development for Allied Van Lines in Naperville, Illinois is quoted as saying, "A great way to keep good people is to do whatever you can to help them grow within your organization." Sieckman informally and formally questions employees about their career direction, then helps them plot their course to get there.

At Honeywell, the company uses a mentoring program to keep their most talented employees. Says Weimerskirch, "Admittedly we aim the mentoring program at our most talented people because they're the ones we most want to keep. The young executive I mentor has the potential to move into the top tier of management at Honeywell. We'd rather he be a senior executive here than somewhere else."

7. ***Educate them***
    Building self-esteem and loyalty as well as the ability to thrive in a marketplace with increasing equipment sophistication, employee education programs offer employees the tools to become more competitive and empowered. Brewer notes the "Noontime University" offered by Einson Freeman, a series of on-site seminars focusing on topics such as direct marketing, research and price promotion.

    "We invest about two percent of our total revenues in education of all forms. People appreciate this because it's another form of income, and knowledge is another form of empowerment," Brewer quotes the Einson Freeman CEO.

The point is that you can't implement any of these ideas, build employee loyalty, or increase employee performance until you can effectively communicate with your employee. And, you can't effectively communicate with your employee if he is worried about having to constantly protect himself. Having to protect themselves requires employees to make excuses and making excuses interferes with real, two-way communication and gets in the way of results.

To get results and improve communications, you first have to get rid of excuses!

In the next chapter we'll define a "No Excuses" culture, why it's important to the company bottom line and how to achieve this empowering culture for your company, its employees and leaders. The concept of a "No Excuses" culture was first identified by Dr. David G. Mutchler and James Bleech, co-authors of *Let's get results, not excuses!* I've found development of a "No Excuses" culture to be absolutely fundamental to building company success -- as vital as the bricks and mortar that are the framework of a building.

Chapter Summary

Key points in this chapter included:

- Hiring and firing employees at will, while rarely an option in the past, is an even less viable alternative today. This makes the ability to motivate and coach employees vitally important.

- Leaders have to respect the technical competence of their employees. This means it's OK to question employees, to have them explain how they intend to perform an assignment. The important point is not to tell them "How" to do their job unless absolutely necessary.

- IBM's rule of seven, that a manager can only effectively manage and control a maximum of seven direct reporting subordinates, is dead and buried. Most supervisors and managers typically have 10 to 15 and sometimes over 20 people reporting to them. This makes delegation and empowerment even more important than in the past.

- To be an effective coach you must first be an active listener. Active listening on the part of the leader/coach satisfies most employees' most common complaints: their bosses do not listen to them.

- Social Scientist Frederick Herzberg has identified the six prime motivators to be:

  1. Achievement - successfully completing an assignment or task.

  2. Recognition of Achievement - a simple word of "Thanks."

  3. The work itself - enjoying what they do.

  4. Responsibility - being empowered.

  5. Advancement - promotions and pay raises or bonuses.

  6. The possibility for growth - the opportunity to learn more and to become more effective at what they do.

  Money does not buy loyalty. Effective coaching inspires loyalty, hard work and creativity.

Notes

Chapter III

Developing A "No Excuses" Culture

> *"If Top Management sets the example there is little need to broadcast the rules"*
>
> *Clark Johnson*

Dr. David Mutchler and James Bleech, in their book *Let's get results, not excuses,* published in 1994 by MVP Press, Grand Rapids, MI, have clearly defined the problem facing nearly every organization and have mapped out a straightforward solution to the challenge of eliminating excuses so the entire organization can focus on results. Their findings are confirmed every time we look at organizations that excel in consistently delivering results. Whether it is a Navy SEAL team, an Army Special Forces team, a highly skilled Research & Development Team or a well-organized and motivated operating room team performing complex surgery, the end results speak for themselves. Creating a "No Excuses" culture is fundamental to effective leadership and coaching.

One of the biggest problems facing almost all executives, managers and supervisors, and the single most frustrating part of the job, is the overwhelming number of excuses they encounter every day. It appears to have become a fact of life that no one is responsible for anything that goes wrong. Not only is it not their fault, it's almost always something that is totally out of their control.

Every company has a culture. Some are planned, meaning that leaders actually took the time to determine what they wanted it to be and may have even written a culture statement, but most company cultures simply take on a life of their own over time. The culture represents how the employees think about the business, what type of business they are in, and how customers are viewed and treated.

The culture also reflects the company's values, how it communicates internally, its standards of performance and virtually everything else that deals with its unconscious, and sometimes conscious, thoughts and feelings relating to business life. Essentially, the culture is a company's personality.

Without a conscious effort to create a culture, it,

more often than not, is based on tradition. This tradition may reflect either the company itself or its key leaders. It's important to remember that the culture is the way things are actually done and how events are actually perceived.

This can be, and in many cases is, in direct conflict with a company's stated policies. This is particularly true in outlying offices or branches. It's quite common to visit a corporate office and find very formal surroundings where employees are required to wear business dress and adhere to a very rigid standard of acceptable behavior. While, in contrast, the branches or field offices are "informal" with very loose work standards. From the outside it's sometimes hard to believe that this is the same company.

I found this to be true in my own experience when I worked for Fortune 500 companies. For example, Caterpillar's headquarters in Peoria, Illinois is a model of professionalism. I remember an incident that occurred during my second week on the job over 22 years ago. I walked into the office bright and early, wearing a navy blue blazer and gray slacks. As I passed one of the division manager's offices, the manager, Dick Zych, gave me a friendly "Good morning" and then asked "Were the lights off in your closet this morning?" I had no idea what he was talking about until one of my peers, who had overheard the comment, told me about the company's unwritten policy concerning suits. The written corporate policy didn't specify wearing suits but the culture was that nothing but a suit, preferably dark in color and conservatively cut, was acceptable attire.

Later, after moving into the field, I found that the appropriate work attire depended more upon the individual manager than upon corporate policy or culture. Some offices carried out the headquarters' tradition of suits, some were a little more relaxed and allowed sport coats (conservative of course) and others were very relaxed with ties as optional dress.

It is the culture that truly reflects how things are done and what are acceptable versus unacceptable standards of behavior or dress as I've just illustrated, even when the culture is in conflict with stated policies.

In another example, while the corporate policy stated that work begins at 7:42 a.m. and ends at 4:12 p.m., the culture "stated" that everyone arrived at work no later than 7:30 a.m., and most of us didn't consider leaving until after 5:30 or 6:00 p.m. Conversely, my experience was almost the opposite when I worked for a multibillion-dollar company headquartered in New York City. When I first arrived I was told that the official starting time was 9:00 a.m., but I quickly found that 9:00 a.m. reflected when people started coming in, not when they actually started working. I learned not to schedule any meetings before 9:30 or 10:00 a.m. if I wanted full attendance from other departments. Culture clearly is stronger than any written policy.

One of the most difficult aspects of a company culture is trying to change it. It usually can't be successfully changed via an edict or new policy. Remember, cultures are stronger than any policy. If you have a problem believing this, just look at the Federal Bureaucracy... it's virtually immune to change.

So how do you change an existing culture that tolerates or even encourages excuses into a "No Excuses" culture? First, remember that the culture is determined by those in leadership positions. The first step to enacting change is for the leader to assume the responsibility for no longer accepting, nor making, excuses. This can be the CEO or the supervisor of a work group. But it has to be the leader!

In virtually every organization, excuse making and acceptance is the default setting. If excuses are not explicitly prohibited they will automatically be assumed to be acceptable.

Before we go any further, go back and reread these two sentences again. This is a critical point and you have to fully understand it if you are going to be successful in establishing a "No Excuses" culture in

47

your section, division, department or company.

The second step is that the leader must declare, verbally, in writing and by action, that excuses are no longer acceptable and that they will be killed at every opportunity. *If this commitment does not exist, then "excusitis" will be the rule of the day!*

To have any chance of success creating and implementing a "No Excuses" culture you have to **explicitly state** that excuses will not be accepted. You not only have to change the default setting, you have to let everyone know that the default setting has been changed. In effect you are stating that your company, department, division or section will have a "No Excuses" culture. You are creating a new set of values for your work group.

What have you done by creating a "No Excuses" culture? *You have set yourself and your employees free to focus on results, not excuses!* You have effectively freed yourself and your employees from the need for self-protection and the fear of retribution. You have allowed your entire team to focus on the results you are seeking and you have empowered your employees to embrace responsibility for their own actions. You have given yourself and your employees the right to be responsible for self-motivation. Most importantly, you have set the stage to allow your employees to accept the responsibility for delivering higher levels of performance by freeing them to use their talents and abilities to do their job to the best of their ability. *You have set the stage, by accepting the responsibility for delivering results, for your own success!*

Excuses are made for anything and everything. In an era when many people feel their jobs are at risk and feel insecure about their and/or their company's future, it's understandable why this is more true today than just a few years ago. But, if left unchecked, "excusitis" will only get in the way of solid communication and coaching. It also gets in the way of results. The truth is, you can only have one -- result or excuse -- *they are mutually exclusive!* So if you accept excuses, you have, by definition, chosen to forfeit results!

The source of the problem is the acceptance of excuses by executives, managers and supervisors instead of focusing on the desired results. **Note what we just said:** *It is not the fault of the employees who make the excuses. It's the fault of the managers who accept them!* Until the "need for excuses" is eliminated and until management is no longer willing to accept excuses, the problem will persist.

The only one who can eliminate the need to make excuses is the leader. Each executive, each manager and each supervisor has the ability to change the culture in his own unit. It doesn't have to be company-wide, though that is the preferred manner.

What we're talking about is a management decision to focus on desired levels of performance instead of faultfinding and finger pointing. This is an "attitude" and a philosophy. But it's one that has to emanate from the top, from the leader, because he or she has the power to punish.

The solution to "excusitis" is actually a two-step process. Both steps must be introduced simultaneously. First, implement a firm "No Excuses" culture in your reporting unit. As I've already mentioned, this does not mean taking a hard-nosed attitude but rather creating a climate where excuses are not needed, nor accepted.

The second step is that you, as the leader, and then your people, your team, must refocus attention on results. This takes a single-minded discipline and may seem not only unnatural but, to some, even threatening because you, as the leader, are voluntarily giving up the power to immediately vent your frustrations by unloading on the employee who fails to meet your expectations and impose immediate punishment. It also means that you, as the leader, have to focus your attention on the desired results instead of faultfinding and finger pointing. However, once your unit understands that what you are doing is focusing on getting the job done, they will begin to loosen up and will willingly become involved.

This is not something that will take hold overnight. It takes time to create and build trust. And, it's only when the employees feel they can trust their leader that they will feel comfortable enough to stop making excuses (when they feel they don't have to protect themselves if something goes wrong). The level of motivation and achievement in an organization can never rise above the level of trust between the employees and their leader. So let me say it again, it is only when employees trust their leaders that they can shift their focus from making excuses to protect themselves to obtaining results.

Developing a "No Excuses" culture is actually harder for the leader. You not only have to discipline yourself against accepting excuses, you also have to stop making them yourself. This is one time when there is no choice but to lead by example. *You have to constantly ferret out excuses and kill them before they take hold!*

How do you do it? Simple, you clearly define the performance level you expect. Then focus on why you and your team are not obtaining these results and what needs to be done to obtain the level of performance, the results, you have established as the goal. The problem is that it's easier to understand this concept than it is to implement it. The hardest part is separating valid reasons from excuses. Frankly, this will always be a matter of opinion and individual determination. The truth is, one person's reason is another person's excuse:

"I couldn't get it on time because the parts weren't available."

Why weren't they available? Did you forget to order them? Was the wrong part ordered? Why was the inventory record wrong? *Find the real reason and you can focus on the results.*

"I couldn't get the unit up on time because I wasn't authorized to work overtime."

Did you have the right tools? Did you have the manual available? Had you pre-ordered the parts? Could you have asked for help earlier? *Find the real reason and you can focus on the results.*

"We're understaffed because Frank's on vacation."

Did you reschedule the routine maintenance to account for vacations? Did you schedule back up or float personnel from other shifts to ensure coverage would be available? Did you consider contracting priority work during vacation periods? *Find the real reason and you can focus on the results.*

"I lost the sale because our price was too high."

Did we build too much into our proposal? Did the customer understand the added value of our on-time delivery and quality guarantees? Did we know the customer's budget parameters and restrictions? *Find the real reason and you can focus on the results.*

The key to stopping excuses and holding people accountable is to know how to differentiate an excuse from a reason.

The Difference Between A Reason And An Excuse Is Control

Who had the ability to control the outcome? If a person stating the "reason" could have, or should have, been able to do something about the outcome, if he could have done something else, *then it's an excuse*, not a reason.

This is a discipline that requires constant emphasis and practice. But it will only work if your employees understand that they are part of the process and won't be punished for telling the truth. *(That's a pretty big "and." <u>Don't Even</u> think of overlooking it or you will lose before you start.)*

The biggest challenge is to educate your employees concerning what they could have or should have done to get the results. They will only be open for this approach if it's presented in a minimal risk environment -- an environment that allows them to openly discuss the options and learn more from their experience. If this environment is not clearly present, you can't get to a "No Excuses" culture!

Stephen Covey *(author of The 7 Habits of Highly Effective People and First Things First)* was quoted in a recent interview: "Often the structures and systems in an organization don't reinforce the principles taught. You're told relationship selling is the key, integrity selling is the key, but the system says, 'Have you made your quota for the month?' To make them all winners, you change the system so that if they accomplish the desired results agreed upon by the sales person and the sales manager, based on conditions of the marketplace, their experience, and their skill level, they win."

Until a "No Excuses" culture exists, it will be virtually impossible to get employees to accept responsibility for their own actions and omissions. This is the foundation of the Coaching Process incorporated in this book.

As the manager, your superiors judge you according to your results. But your employees judge you on your integrity and consistency. Real leaders deliver results while maintaining integrity and consistency. You must set the tone for your work group whether it's a small unit, a department or the entire company.

As Covey points out in *The 7 Habits of Highly Effective People,* having a powerful sense of purpose, integrity and empathy is the only way to be successful in business and in life. For instance, he states in Habit No. 1: "Be proactive. Your actions should be based on deeply held principles, not fleeting moods, feelings, and circumstances." In Habit No. 2, he stresses beginning with the end in mind and advocates a personal mission statement (or company culture statement) that spells out the meaning, purpose and direction of your personal or business life. (A sample culture statement is included at the end of this chapter.)

He says in Habit No. 5, "seek first to understand, then to be understood" or approach all relationships with a high level of empathy.

Show your employees you're interested in them -- that the norm is *truthful,* two-way communication. Give them the opportunity to critique you about your

job.   In   one   fast-rising   Florida-based   company,
employees   have   the   opportunity   to   evaluate   their
managers,   resulting   in   the   possible   demotion   of   a
supervisor. Contrary to what you might think, this is
not a threatening environment but rather a truthful
exchange of information. No one loses his job, unless
his or her attitude and performance remain unchanged
and it becomes obvious that the manager is not capable
of transitioning into a leader. Even then, the manager
is placed in an area where he is thought to be the most
productive.

As Wilfred Calmas, president of Sales Growth
Unlimited, a consulting firm in Boston notes: "Too
many managers are inflexible when it comes to giving
feedback to their salespeople" *(or vice versa for fear of
retribution).*   This   can   be   said   of   all   too   many
managers in all departments and levels throughout
most organizations.   But is this not the primary role
and responsibility of virtually every manager? Isn't the
ability to provide effective feedback, both positive and
negative, to employees of utmost importance to getting
the job done?

Coaching requires trust. As you will see in
following chapters, employees must feel comfortable
and unthreatened or the process can't work. They will
feel that they have to make excuses.

Sample Sales & Marketing Culture Statement:

Our sales and marketing department is a proactive, aggressive business development team focused on developing new business opportunities and long-term partnerships concentrating on medium and large employers in industries where confidentiality and integrity are integral to their success.

Our sales and marketing department is results oriented and embraces and lives by its "No Excuses" Culture by focusing on results and refusing to allow faultfinding or finger pointing. Our sales and marketing department is committed to team selling and includes regional program specialists, national account managers, plant operations, customer service managers, corporate administrators and vendors as valuable members of our sales team, all with a vital role to play.

Chapter Summary

Key points in this chapter included:

- Every company and every department within a company has a culture. Some are planned but most simply evolve over time.

- Cultures are stronger than written policies, they reflect how things really are, not how some administrator, bureaucrat or executive would like it to be.

- It is extremely difficult to change a culture but it can be done. Only a leader can change a culture.

- Creating a "No Excuses" Culture requires two distinct steps by the leader:

  Step 1 - The leader must accept the responsibility of no longer accepting or making excuses. The leader must declare verbally, in writing and by action that excuses are no longer acceptable and will be killed at every opportunity. The leader must change the default setting to "NO Excuses".

  Step 2 - The leader must refocus his/her attention, and the attention of his subordinates, on results.

- Creating a "No Excuses" culture sets yourself and your employees free to focus on results... not excuses.

- Creating a "No Excuses" culture sets the stage for allowing employees to accept the responsibility of delivering results and their own success.

- A culture that accepts excuses is not the fault of the employee that makes excuses, it is the fault of the manager who accepts them.

- The only person who can eliminate the need to make excuses is the leader.

- Creating a "No Excuses" culture takes time. It takes time to create and build trust. It is only when employees feel they can trust their leader that they will stop making excuses.

- The difference between a reason and an excuse is control. If the person stating the "reason" could have or should have been able to do something about the outcome, if he could have done something else, *then it's an excuse*, not a reason.

- A "No Excuses" culture cannot be implemented if employees fear they will be punished for telling the truth.

- Until a "No Excuses" culture exists, it will be virtually impossible to get employees to accept responsibility for their own actions and omissions.

Notes

Chapter IV

The Solution: Effective Coaching

> *"We seldom take time to show people what we need, but we are disappointed when they don't deliver."*
> *Alan Williams*

To become an effective coach you first have to become a "No Excuses" Leader. It is a process. This means there is a defined way of doing it and each step must be completed, in order -- every time. Because it is a process, there's a road map to follow.

There are two distinct phases. The first phase is the upfront or initial coaching session. This includes the following four steps:

1)   Tell 'em what you want... Be specific

2)   Tell 'em "Why"... Not "How"

3)   Identify possible problems... Develop Contingencies

4)   Identify potential resources... Who are your "Parachute Packers"

The second phase is the follow-up and feedback process, which is appropriately called:

5)   Follow-up... and follow through.

Following these five steps will make every coaching session a success.

Each Phase Must Be Used Regularly And Consistently

Caution: Expect employee skepticism at the beginning. Until they see you, the manager/leader, living a "No Excuses" attitude, and see consistency in your use of the coaching process, many will see it as just one more management or behavioral fad. The best results will be obtained if managers first practice and commit to the process with their direct subordinates, especially first-line supervisors and lead people. Take it a step at a time. Don't try to rush too fast. However, let your employees know you're serious about implementing this process and let them see you embrace it yourself. Once they see you living a "No Excuses" philosophy, living the process and they get used to your coaching style, they will accept it. One method that has worked for me is to ask for volunteers. All you need is one or two to demonstrate the effectiveness of the process. Once this group has fully bought-in and used the process they can take it to the next level in the organization.

The first step in getting the buy-in for the re-engineering of a management process is convincing your employees that it is good for the organization -- and for them. Involving one or two key employees in the process early on by notifying them of planned changes, getting their feedback, and including them in process work, is the key to gaining acceptance.

This process works with customers and prospects just as well as with employees. This same strategy holds true if your employees are under-performing and your bottom line is suffering as a result. Go to them for feedback. This will create high morale and increased cooperation. Remember what was said earlier about the number one complaint of most employees, "The unwillingness of supervisors and managers to listen to them." By listening to your employees you not only gain valuable insight into the problem, you also stand to gain a better understanding of possible solutions. Most importantly, you are re-establishing the rules of the game and are beginning the implementation of a "No Excuses" culture and effective coaching.

Taking an example from sales and the need to turn-around competitive losses, Andy Cohen writes in "Just Fix It, your sales process that is" (*Sales & Marketing Management*, September 1996), "When sales go south, it's time not just to evaluate the performance of individual salespeople, but to take a hard look at the company's entire sales process -- the complex procedures and systems from acquiring a lead, to closing a sale, to following-up with the customer. Individual salespeople can only do so much. They need to work in a system that helps them succeed." By seeking the input of the entire organization, listening to their input and suggestions, he was able to redesign the entire sales process. By including the employees and incorporating their input, employee buy-in and ownership was assured.

Whether it's your sales, operations, distribution, accounting or any other department, the key to successful reengineering and effective turnarounds is employee involvement in identifying the problem and creating new or improved processes.

When IBM suffered a downfall several years

ago, it was the restructuring of its sales force and, most importantly, its *sales process* that brought it back.

The point being made is that regardless of what department the leader is responsible for, more often than not it's either the lack of effective processes or a failure to follow the proscribed process that is responsible for the failure of obtaining desired results. Yet most managers hang the blame on their employees. The truth is, even the best employees cannot consistently deliver extraordinary results if they lack an effective process.

This is why leaders need a process for coaching. Knowing "Why" he/she should coach is only part of the equation. A leader has to know "How" to coach.

The coaching process advocated here provides the technique needed to get the entire organization focused on delivering extraordinary results.

In subsequent chapters, I will explain each step of the coaching process to give you a tactical plan for achieving the results you want. The solution to the problems which many companies face is the implementation of "No Excuses" leadership and effective coaching to obtain employee buy-in and cooperation. By following the coaching process detailed in the following chapters you'll gain the acceptance and cooperation of your employees. It doesn't make any difference what division or department you're working with. The process works equally well in engineering, maintenance, accounting, shipping, research and development, marketing or sales. But it takes a leader to put it in place.

Chapter Summary

Key points in this chapter included:

- Breaking the coaching process into two distinct phases:

- The first phase is the upfront, or initial, coaching session and consists of the first four steps:

    1)   Tell 'em what you want... Be specific.

    2)   Tell 'em "Why"... not "How."

    3)   Identify possible problems... Develop Contingencies.

    4)   Identify potential resources... Identify your "Parachute Packers."

The second phase is the follow-up and feedback process:

    5)   Follow-up and follow through... Make every coaching process a success.

- As with any other process, each step must be followed in order and consistently applied for it to work.

- When any organization incurs problems it is more often the case that they either lack an effective process or are failing to follow a process. Fixing the process, or developing a proven process, is the key to consistently delivering extraordinary results. More often than not, the problem is the process, not the people.

Notes

Chapter V

Step 1: Tell 'em What You Want... *Be Specific*

> *"Be specific when describing the performance you want – get to ground level instead of 40,000 feet."*
>
> *Jerry Jellison*

The warden in the movie *Cool Hand Luke* said it best: "What we have here is a failure to communicate." But whose fault is it? It really doesn't matter! What matters is who will take the responsibility to change the situation. The manager/leader needs to step up to the plate and take responsibility for ensuring communication does take place. This is a top-down process and the coach has to assume responsibility for making it work -- **No Excuses!**

The first step of the coaching process is to: "Tell 'em what you want... be specific." What do you want accomplished? What defines the difference between marginal, acceptable and superior performance? How does the employee know, in clear, unmistakable terms, whether he has succeeded or failed? All too often a sales representative, supervisor, manager or craft worker doesn't know exactly what's expected of him or her. It's no wonder he expresses surprise and, typically, also anger, when told he's under performing.

Without a benchmark of expectation, there is no clear method of evaluation. Mike Ragan, North American sales manager of Waterproofing Products for W.R. Grace, in Cambridge, Massachusetts, developed a benchmark by first profiling the company's top performers. He asked questions such as: how many calls they make per day, what they said to customers, how they built relationships and their level of knowledge. This became the expected level of performance for all sales representatives. This became a defined standard that management and employees could use to identify acceptable vs. unacceptable performance. ("Person to Person: Lighting a fire under average performers," *Sales & Marketing Management*, January 1996.)

A benchmark of expectation sets the stage for the first step of coaching for buy-in and results which is to make sure you and your employee are not only in the same book but are also on the same page. You have to not only communicate your expectation or expectations but be 100 percent sure that the person who is being coached fully understands what you expect as an outcome.

To work, it's absolutely essential that the employee repeat, in his own words, what he "thinks he heard you say." Don't be surprised if the employee heard something other than what you think you said! (This is why effective communication is a two-way street.)

This requires that you, as the coach, clearly define what you want accomplished. You have to clearly state what your goal is in specific terms. Ideally these terms should be in the form of something that can be measured... Either you got what you asked for or you did not. How will you and the employee being coached know if he or she is successful? If the employee cannot state in his own words what you want he will have little chance of delivering it.

Have the person you're coaching tell you how he defines success. Keep talking and working on a shared definition of success until you reach a clear understanding of what success means to both of you. This may involve establishing a standard three-level goal approach that defines what you both agree to be *the minimal goal, the primary goal* and *the visionary goal.*

The Minimal Goal is the least that is expected and still be considered a success. In sales, this is often nothing more than gaining new information or a new insight into the prospect's need(s). In plant maintenance, it might be getting a machine back up and running within a reasonable time limit. In a hospital, it might mean having all medications properly dispensed and charted on schedule. In manufacturing, it might mean meeting the production schedule with the minimum defects allowed. Regardless of what it is, the coach and employee need to both agree on the minimal acceptable standard and both need to understand that failure to meet even this minimum standard will be considered unacceptable performance.

The Primary Goal is the level of performance the coach actually expects. The employee is expected to attain this level of performance. In sales, it could be getting on the approved bidder list or being given the opportunity to provide a quote. In plant maintenance, it could mean diagnosing the cause of a failure, getting the machine up and running and completing the work order documentation within the allotted or estimated time. In the hospital, it could be administering medications, taking vital signs, and charting and responding to patient requests within the scheduled time. In manufacturing, it

76

could be meeting the production schedule with zero defects. Again, the specifics must be understood by both the coach and the employee and both must agree that the expectations are realistic and attainable.

The Visionary Goal is the optimum level of performance that can reasonably be anticipated. In sales, it could be obtaining a non-solicited order or an opportunity to bid in a new area. In plant maintenance, it could be not just failure diagnosis and repair but the creation of a new maintenance procedure to prevent future failures. Regardless of the discipline, the coach and employee must define what they expect and what they will accept as a "visionary" goal accomplishment.

Let's put this in the form of a simple example. It's 7:00 a.m. and you have a long drive to your 10:00 a.m. appointment. You have been having problems with your battery and now it's dead. It will not take a charge and you cannot jump-start the car. You need a new battery. You give your son $100.00 and tell him to buy a new battery, but to try and find one that costs less than $65.

What happens if the son shops around and finds the battery you want for $55 but doesn't get back until after 9:30 a.m., too late for you to make it to your

10:00 a.m. appointment. Was he successful? It depends on whose expectation or perception is involved. For both the coach (the father) and the subordinate (the son) to share the same expectation of success, they have to both understood what is expected. Whose fault is it if the son didn't know he had to be back by 9:00 for the father to have time to make his 10:00 appointment? Would the father see his son's effort as successful if he spent $80 but was back in time for his appointment? Probably. Would the son be successful if he was able to buy the battery for $50 and still make it back in time for the father to make his appointment. Absolutely. Here the son has accomplished the optimal or visionary goal.

The key is to achieve clear communication. To work, both the sender and the receiver -- the coach and the employee -- must share a common vision of the goals/objectives. This is an absolute that must exist before moving on to the next step. Make no mistake about it though, ensuring a clear understanding is absolutely the responsibility of the coach, not the employee... **No Excuses**.

"Expectation management," making sure your employee knows exactly what you expect and want, is the hallmark of a good coach. Making sure employees stay focused on their objective and always beginning with constructive feedback are also vital coaching tactics.

When in the field on sales calls, one sales coach suggests finding a reason to praise your representative in front of the customer. And, after the call is completed, to communicate your observations on a positive note.

The W.S. Reed Company, an office products maker in Grand Rapids, Michigan has a "formula for success" it has used for 38 years. By profiling its top performers, company officials developed a job description which they share with prospective representatives and, in some cases, have them initial it "so we know we're in agreement -- that this is a job they can see themselves doing successfully," says Russ Reed, vice president and general manager.

The six-step job description clearly communicates the company's high standards and performance expectations to new salespeople ("Start at the Beginning," *Sales & Marketing Management*, March 1996):

1)   Objectives/Goals

2)   Leadership

3)   Professional Development

4)   Account Responsibility

5)   Customer Responsibility

6)   Business Account Responsibility

In the following chapter we'll discuss Step 2 of the Coaching Process, Tell' em "Why" ... Not "How". In our example of the father, the son and the failed car battery, the father communicated his expectations -- he won if the son successfully purchased the battery for under $60 and was back in time for his appointment. The son's expectations for success were also defined. He "won" when he successfully purchased the battery and was back at the predetermined hour. But what was his reward? Was the end result communicated and his errand rewarded with one of Herzberg's six prime motivators: achievement, recognition of achievement, the work itself, responsibility, advancement, or, the possibility for growth.

Chapter Summary

Key points in this chapter included:

- It is the coach's responsibility to clearly define the goal... <u>exactly</u> what is expected.

- Define goals in measurable, terms... be specific.

- Use a standard three-level goal (MPV).

  <u>Minimum</u>-What is the very least you will accept? Clearly define failure as well as success.

  <u>Primary</u>-What is the level of achievement you expect.

  <u>Visionary</u>-What is the optimal level of performance that can reasonably be anticipated.

- Have the employee, the person being coached, tell you in his or her own words what they understand the goal to be. Keep working on it until both the coach and the person being coached agree on what constitutes success, <u>and failure.</u>

Notes

Chapter VI

Step 2: Tell'em "Why"...
Not "How"

> *"The first Rule of engagement... Incoming rounds have the right of way."*
>
> *Special Forces, Special Operations Group*
> *Handbook on Survival in Combat*

Successful coaching requires a "win-win" relationship. "Win-win" has become an overused term and has lost much of its original meaning. For the purposes of this book, I will take the liberty of defining "win-win." As it's used here, it means that the coach gets what he wants... the employee performing to his level of expectation and contributing to the achievement of the established goals and objectives. For the employee, it means that he gets what he wants... he is being listened to and at least one of the prime motivators, identified by Frederick Herzberg and listed in Chapter II, is satisfied. But this doesn't mean you have to offer a special *spif,* bonus or favor for every action. Sometimes, "what's in it for them," is nothing more than that the employee gets to keep his job. The goal is for him to do his own job better, more consistently or to simply take his turn at an unpleasant task. But in every coaching situation the coach has the opportunity to help the employee understand his or her role and importance as a member of the team.

Going back to our example of the father, the son and the battery, what the son may get out of helping his father is the privilege of using the car that night. Or, he may be rewarded with other forms of recognition for his accomplishment as well as the satisfaction of a job well done. But he also gets to know and understand his importance to the father's success and what that means to the family.

Regardless of what approach you take as a coach, you need to always be sure to include this step, Tell 'em "Why"... Make sure they understand the reason they are being asked to do something or to change a behavior. Until the person being coached understands the "Why," they cannot buy-into and accept the need to do a task or change a behavior. It is nearly impossible to coach without some forethought. It is dangerous and foolhardy to "wing it," particularly at the beginning of your development as a coach. Your employees will see right through your lack of preparation. If they see you haven't taken the time to prepare yourself for this discussion, they are apt to conclude that you're either not serious about the process or simply don't think it's important enough to spend the time to properly prepare yourself. There is also the danger that they could interpret your lack of preparation to mean that they are not important, and are not worth your time and the effort it takes to make them part of the team.

This also may be the time to reiterate career path requirements and how, by doing what the coach expects, the employee will have an opportunity to move ahead. This isn't being manipulative. It's making sure the employee understands the advantages of doing his job to the best of his ability.

This step is most effective if the employee is given the opportunity and, if necessary, required to identify for himself "what's in it for him." Ask the questions:

1) "What do *you* think are the primary advantages to you for reaching the goals?"

2) "What will *you* get out of this?"

85

3) "What will accomplishing this goal do for our organization?"

More times than not your employee will bring up the best reasons, probably reasons you would not have anticipated.

Let your employees know what's expected of them by coaching them to become stars. Spend adequate time in advance of the coaching session to think through each step to determine what you want included and what you need to guard against. The danger is allowing yourself to be maneuvered into accepting a quid pro quo from the employee who wants specific recognition or favors for meeting the desired goal. The coach must take the time to think through the obstacles he may be forced to deal with during the coaching session. Taking the time to plan in advance is critical to the success of this process.

There is sometimes a temptation to skip the preparation stage when time is short, to enter the coaching session "on the fly." This would be a mistake. In my experience, even the most expert coaches take a minute before they start the process to think it through and make sure they know why they want someone to perform a specific task, change a behavior or accept an assignment. This technique is how good coaches prevent having to make excuses.

In Special Forces training the instructors would constantly tell us (typically by screaming) to "overcome and improvise." The only way this can be effectively done is to initiate some preplanning to include contingency planning. During training exercises we had to turn in our operations plans, and as we progressed the instructors also had us submit our contingency plans. They then would turn our plans over to the aggressor force, the unit that acted as our enemy. With our plans in hand they were in a position to defeat us every time.

We quickly learned to have multiple contingency plans available, even if they weren't formalized or written down. This helped us quickly review our alternatives so we could more readily react to overcome and improvise as the situation dictated. This is no different than what the coach must do to be ready to handle curve balls that might be thrown by an employee who might try to take advantage of the situation or who is uncooperative, or even recalcitrant.

In this step, Tell 'em "Why" not "How" -- it's more often than not the "Big Picture" and how the person being coached impacts it that makes the biggest difference. Napoleon was famous for many reasons, but one of his lesser-known accomplishments was his impact on motivating and rewarding combat troops. He was one of the first to recognize the importance of unit integrity and how, by keeping fighting units together he and his commanders could motivate their troops to endure hardships and danger for the betterment of the unit. He was the first combat leader to use the threat of being removed from their unit as a punishment. He was the first leader to offer unit citations as well as individual medals.

One of the most important aspects of this step is to offer the employees an understanding of their value to the team and the organization.

Research about employee satisfaction has repeatedly shown that the two complaints most often cited by employees about their work are:

1)   They feel they don't make a difference; their work isn't important.

2)   They feel they aren't part of the team; they aren't important.

These complaints aren't limited to just the people on the shop floor, they're reiterated at virtually every level of the organization.

This step of the process not only helps gain buy-in, it also helps the coach create a real team, building true esprit de corps. By moving the focus from the individual who is being coached to the team, his work group, and the company, the employee is able to gain insight into his importance to the organization and the importance of the job he is doing.

When people understand that what they are doing has value and that they are important to the team's mission, they will want to get the results.

In the example of the father sending his son out for a battery, if he doesn't communicate to his son that he has an appointment at 10 o'clock, the son won't understand the importance of getting back on time. If the father doesn't communicate this, then how can he expect his son to understand why getting back on time is more important than continuing to shop in order to save a few dollars?

So, whose responsibility is it to insure understanding exists?   The Coach!

You don't have to be melodramatic, but you do have to provide the other person with a clear under- standing of the importance of the assignment and how others will be affected by the results.

Communicating the "why" can be as simple as showing the employee a critical path flow chart of the project and the effect that failing to complete an assignment on time will have on the entire project. The key to the process is to share information and to clearly communicate what you know so the other person -- the one you are coaching -- shares your understanding. Clearly state the importance of the following:

1) What you want them to do

2) When you want it done

3) The parameters and guidelines that apply

Without this shared understanding, the door for future excuses is left wide open! The added value of this step of the coaching process is making the person you're coaching part of the team.

As Vince Lombardi used to say: "It's not the runner's job to get the ball across the goal line... it's the entire team's job."

Sometimes this step is difficult if the task is routine. It can appear inconsequential or unimportant. Employees quickly identify a non-issue when it's presented. In the real world it's extremely difficult, if not impossible, to make the mundane important.

But communicating the "Why" is not inconsequential! Every small improvement makes a significant difference in a very short time. A ½ percent improvement every week amounts to a 26 percent improvement in a single year!   Even if the improvement is only 20 percent in a year, that percentage is extremely important and extremely valuable to the team, organization and company.

Small improvements are the heart of Kaizen, the Japanese management principle of continuous improvement. The concept of Kaizen is that small improvements, made continuously over a long period of time, can radically reshape and improve processes. In many cases, this is the "Why!"

The popularity of this management tool took off in the late '70s and early '80s at about the same time as total quality management, TQM. The difference between the two is one of philosophy versus technicality.

Thought to be a personal TQM, one characteristic of the concept is the constant search-and-destroy mission of rooting out mistakes (which parallels the "No Excuses" coaching process, where leaders and coaches are constantly on the lookout for excuses). The focus is one of process improvement rather than results improvement. And, similarly, one of system improvement as opposed to individual improvement.

Like the "No Excuses" culture described in Chapter III, the emphasis of *Kaizen* is not one of faultfinding or blame, but instead one of future opportunity. What can be learned from the situation or result and projected to a better outcome in the future?

In Chapter VII, Step 3: "Identify Possible Problems... Develop Contingencies," we'll talk about the most important step in effective coaching. This is the method for ferreting out excuses before they occur so you will achieve your goals and objectives.

Chapter Summary

Key points in this chapter included:

- Successful coaching is always a win-win scenario.

- Effective coaching requires planning and forethought. The coach has to know what his employee's win is going to be. The employee may realize additional "wins" beyond those identified by the coach -- but only if he's asked to identify them.

- Employees are motivated by two distinct reward systems -- personal rewards, i.e., "What's in it for me" and inclusionary or contributory rewards, i.e., the "Big Picture," and contributing to the team. More often than not it is the "Big Picture" that is the primary motivator. Napoleon is quoted as saying, "No man ever dies for his country. He dies for the Medals." Napoleon also proved that soldiers (sic employees) are primarily motivated by their intense desire to support their buddy, their unit and the mission. This is the "Big Picture."

- The coach must focus on the "Why" if he wants employee buy-in; an employee must understand why before buy-in is possible. Let the employee focus on the how after he understands the why.

- The two most frequently identified employee complaints are:

  1) They feel they don't make a difference; that their work isn't important.

  2) They feel they aren't part of the team; that they aren't important.

  Focusing on the "Why" satisfies both of these concerns.

- Even inconsequential and routine tasks can have an important "why" if the focus is on continuous improvement... Kaizen. This is why a "No Excuses" culture is critical to effective coaching. It is only when the entire team is focused on continuous improvement and eliminating excuses that a coach can focus on "Why" and let the employee focus on "How."

Notes

Chapter VII

Step 3: Identify Possible Problems... Develop Contingencies

> *"If we feel committed, when there is a problem we look for solutions... if not, we look for a way out."*
> *Zeig Zeigler*

Step 2 of the process, Tell 'em "Why"... Not "How," is the vehicle for obtaining buy-in: commitment. Step 3 of the process is where the coach and the employee look for solutions.

As the Goodyear ad says: "This is where the rubber meets the road." By far, this is the most important step in the process. This is what generates results and eliminates excuses. During this step you, as the leader and coach, have to get the employee to identify all the possible reasons something could go wrong while seeking to accomplish the agreed upon result.

The operative words here are *employee* and *all*. The employee has to do the talking at this stage. The coach's job is to facilitate his input. It **is not** the coach's job to identify even one thing that could go wrong. To get the employee to understand and learn from the coaching process, he or she, the employee, must identify what could go wrong.

The only way he can identify what can go wrong is to think about it. It's the mental process that makes this step important and it's what makes it work. The employee must participate. The coach's job is to facilitate by asking questions and to ensure the employee identifies **everything** that could go wrong. This is an exhaustive process but it is critical to the success of the coaching process. This step makes contingency planning possible.

Shortcutting This Step... Guarantees Failure!

Did that statement get your attention? I don't make this statement lightly. Failure to get the employee to participate in this step of the process guarantees that excuses will crop up and that the goal will not be realized.

The number one reason for failure at this stage is that the coach does the talking. Even if the coach identifies every possible excuse or potential reason for failure, the employee will fail to identify with the problem. He won't own the problem so he can't own the solution.

I can't say it any clearer: It is absolutely critical that the employee does the talking at this stage. The employee must be the one to identify potential reasons for failure and excuses.

Let me tell a story that illustrates the critical importance of contingency planning and its values.

On January 8, 1970 I was in Northern Laos operating with the 5th Special Forces Group (Airborne), Special Operations Group (SOG) when I was captured and taken prisoner as a POW. Prior to starting this mission we planned each step in great detail and developed a wide range of contingencies for just about every conceivable event including the possibility of capture and escape. As a 20-year-old 2nd Lt. in my second tour and with several similar successful missions completed, I was convinced that I was not only more than six feet tall but that I was bullet proof as well. I was confident of my own abilities and those of my team... nevertheless, my commander, my coach, insisted that we develop detailed contingencies with alternate pick-up points and recognition signals that could be used with and without radio contact.

When I was first captured I went through extreme depression and did not even think of escaping. But when the opportunity presented itself, all of my previous training kicked in and I took off. But getting away was the easy part. If I hadn't been forced to develop my own contingency plans for this very eventuality, I would have stumbled around and would have eventually been recaptured. Instead, once I was safely away and hidden, I knew what I had to do and how to do it. Because my commander, my coach, forced me to identify potential failures and to develop my own contingency plans, I not only was prepared to execute them when the need arose, so were all the people involved, my "parachute packers," with helping me get out. (I'll explain this term in the next chapter.)

This may be an extreme example but it fully represents the value and importance of having the person being coached identify, for themselves, every possible cause of failure and then develop a response, a contingency plan.

How does the coach facilitate this step? By asking questions. If the employee has a difficult time developing a list, the coach can play "let's pretend"... what might you tell me is the reason you didn't succeed? The coach can also ask the employee to identify all the reasons (excuses) he has used in the past when he didn't succeed nor do his best.

Some of the possible "excuses" for not accomplishing the objective in the story of the father and son might be that the son, as long as he was going out, stopped to look for a new CD or, that he ran out of gas, or a tire went flat.

Preventative measures would include the understanding that the son should shop for a new CD after purchasing the battery and delivering it to his father. And, that he fills the gas tank before purchasing the battery as well as checking for a spare tire in the trunk.

The key is to have the person who is being coached develop his own list of possible glitches that could prevent goal achievement, and the corrective measures to meet each challenge. This is what creates ownership and buy-in of both the problem and the solution: *experience has shown, all too often, that the person being coached doesn't buy-in unless he's developed his own cause-and-effect scenario.*

When the employee has identified everything that could go wrong and has also developed his own contingencies, then the coach and the employee are both focused on results and have eliminated the need for excuses.

Chapter Summary

Key points in this chapter included:

- The <u>only</u> way this step can effectively be implemented is if the employee does the talking, identifying the potential problems and developing his own contingencies.

- The coach's job is to ask questions; to facilitate the employee's thinking process.

- The only way an employee can "own" the solution is to "own" the problem. The only way an employee can "own" the problem is if he or she identifies the potential problem himself.

- An effective way of coaching this step includes asking questions and playing "let's pretend."

Notes

Chapter VIII

Step 4: Identify Potential Resources... Who Are Your "Parachute Packers?"

> *"No plan survives its collision with reality."*
> *Herb Meyer*

In this step the employee identifies all the resources available to him should he need help. Again, it is critical that the employee develops his own "Parachute Packer." Each employee must identify the books, manuals, coworkers, vendors, etc. that can be used if he runs into trouble.

With permission, I've taken the term "Parachute Packer" from one of the very best motivational speakers I've had the opportunity to listen to, J. Charles Plumb. Charlie Plumb was a 24-year-old "Top Gun" Fighter Pilot flying combat missions off the deck of the U.S. Kitty Hawk when, just seven days short of finishing his tour and rotating back home, he was shot down over North Vietnam and taken as a POW. After six torturous years he was finally released and returned home.

Charlie tells a great story about eating dinner in a restaurant shortly after his return when someone he had never met came up to him and asked if he wasn't Lt. Charles Plumb who had been shot down over North Vietnam. When Charlie acknowledged that he was the same person, the man identified himself as the sailor who had packed his parachute all those many years before.

Totally unknown to the high profile pilots on the flight deck, he was one of the sailors who labored far below the water line doing their jobs to the best of their ability everyday. He was one of those people who you only come to recognize and appreciate in an emergency.

Charlie Plumb's story is much more than this but I believe he has captured the idea, the very concept, of the level of support available to all of us if we just open our eyes to the opportunities and those willing to help. "Parachute Packers" are the people we can count on to help us out with advice, a helping hand or whatever it takes to reverse a bad situation or get us through hard times. "Parachute Packers" are our most valued resources, regardless of their position within the organization. These are the people that make results possible.

Most of us tend to look only to our peers for help. But a "Parachute Packer" does not have to be a peer. It's important that the coach encourage the employee to look at the entire organization for possible resources.

Ideally, the employee should identify separate "Parachute Packers" for each reason viewed as a possible impediment to success. Most times though, you won't have to carry this to the nth degree; the employee will find that many "Parachute Packers" will overlap two or more potential problems. However, the first two or three times this process is used, it's best to take the extra time to identify as many "Parachute Packers" as possible. This will enable the employee to concentrate on finding his own solutions and resources for potential problems *before* they become problems.

In our example of the father and son, some of the "Parachute Packers" for the son might be the parts department at the car dealership or auto parts store. Given enough time, there are an infinite number of possible alternatives.

In a work environment, a "Parachute Packer" might be a more experienced person in the department, or someone with specific skills. But a "Parachute Packer" might also be a helper for the senior craftsman. For an executive, his or her most effective "Parachute Packer" is his or her administrative assistant. In a Parts Department, the Department Manager's most valuable "Parachute Packer" might be the Inventory Control Manager. "Parachute Packers" can be superiors, subordinates, peers or even technical resources.

Identifying potential resources is more than just people that can help. It also includes identifying needed tools, equipment and technical resources required to ensure success. For example, for a maintenance mechanic it might mean ensuring he has all the tools and parts needed and also all the technical manuals, schematics and drawings. For an engineer, it might mean having code books and other technical manuals needed to complete a project.

Identifying potential resources means looking for both the people and things needed to ensure success, a result, and not another excuse.

Making The Coaching Process Work

Like all habits, it will take time for both the coach and the employee to become comfortable with this process. Accept that it will feel a little awkward at first. Be up-front with the employee who is being coached and don't be afraid to use a "cheat sheet" with the process laid out step by step. Feel free to actually lay the whole process out on a sheet of paper with specific questions and possible solutions. Also consider laying out a list of possible excuses for Step 3: Identify possible problems... develop contingencies and another list for Step 4: Identify potential resources... who are your "Parachute Packers," to be sure they are included by the employee.

Effective coaching is only part of the process. Once the assignment is completed, the coaches must follow-up and follow through to ensure continuous success over a period of time. In Chapter IX, we'll "make it a habit" with a proven follow-up and follow through process to ensure every coaching session is a success.

Chapter Summary

Key points in this chapter included:

- As in Step 3, the employee must do the talking, he must think through each possible cause of failure and identify resources, "Parachute Packers," that can help get him back on track.

- Resources can be people, "Parachute Packers," or things such as manuals, policies, procedures, tooling and equipment, etc...

- The coach's job is to facilitate the process, to guide the employee through the thought process.

- Coaches should feel comfortable developing a written plan in advance of the coaching session. There should be no hesitation in allowing the employee to know the coach is following a defined process and that he has taken the time to think through and write out his questions in advance.

Notes

Chapter IX

Step 5: Follow-up...Follow-Through

"Focus on changing behavior, not people."
Peter Schutz

Like anything in life, simply trying something once or twice never results in long-term success. Just as a batter practices his swing over and over and just as a quarterback practices position and timing patterns over and over, leaders must understand they will need continual practice to develop their coaching skills. It is the consistent application of the coaching process that will make it possible for leaders to successfully aid employees in developing the skills they need to make

113

this concept work for you, them and the company. Just as you need time and practice to master this coaching process, your employees also need time and practice to master the new skills, concepts and techniques they're being coached in.

A proven technique for making effective coaching a habit for you and your employees is this simple follow-up approach to be used after each assignment in which a coaching session is involved. The key is to minimize the fear of failure. Although this process will generate greater results and eliminate "excusitis," it cannot guarantee success every time. However, over time, if effectively and continuously implemented, it will move you toward this goal.

First: Review the results

Did the employee do what you told them to do? Did they meet your minimal, primary or visionary goal level? This is where the old management adage, "What you don't measure, you can't manage" proves to be totally correct.

It's important that you start by asking the employee to answer this question: "Did you succeed or fail?" Judge your response by the employee's input. In many cases, especially after the coaching process has been in use for awhile, you will find the employee becomes a harsher critic of success than you are. But, regardless of the outcome, it's critical that you and the employee agree on whether your minimal, primary or visionary goals were met. The worst case scenario is for you to feel the goals were not met while the employee feels they were. If this happens, it is your responsibility to ensure clear communication and a clear understanding of the expectation(s). When addressing this question, focus solely on the desired result, the specific goal. This is not the time to find fault or to even question why the goals were not met. *There can be absolutely no faultfinding at this stage!*

However, if all goals were met, then it's entirely appropriate to provide positive reinforcement for even small successes.

In the example of the father and son, did the son get back with the battery on time? Was he able to get the battery for less than $60? Reviewing results is a simple yes or no situation. Either we achieved the desired results or we didn't. It's absolutely critical that you don't accept any form of excuse or explanation at this time.

Second: Determine if the employee succeeded or learned something

If the desired results were obtained, acknowledge the accomplishment and reinforce the value of the success and the employee's achievement by asking him to review, briefly, why he or she felt he was successful. This should be a detailed summation of the steps he took to ensure success and the anticipated contingencies he encountered. Should the employee identify a contingency actually encountered, it is extremely important to reinforce and congratulate the employee for successfully thinking ahead and correctly anticipating the potential difficulty.

But what if the employee wasn't successful? What if he failed to meet your minimal goal or, if this is a repeated session, the employee is continuing to achieve only the minimal accepted goal or performance level? In this case, you must challenge him to identify at least one lesson learned!

If the desired result was not obtained, then the person who is being coached must tell his coach what happened. This is *not* making an excuse, but factually reviewing the circumstances and identifying what he failed to anticipate or actions that could have either been avoided or taken. This step is critically important. If done right, the coach and the employee will clearly define controllable events and circumstances to prevent the employee from making excuses and the coach from accepting them.

When done correctly, this is when the employee and the coach are able to identify corrective actions, such as a change in a procedure, new or different tooling support requirements, etc., needed for improvement. By eliminating excuses, actively listening and effectively coaching, leaders are able to identify organizational changes needed to improve efficiency, effectiveness and success.

The key here is for the coach to actively listen, with an open mind, and for the employee to offer suggestions on what's needed for him to consistently reach the primary goals. What is clearly obvious is that this can only occur if mutual trust exists between the coach and the employee. That is why it is absolutely critical to start this step of the coaching process with a simple review of the results: was the goal successfully achieved or not, and why neither an excuse nor an explanation is offered or accepted at that time.

Using the battery example, perhaps the son didn't get back in time because he had a flat tire on the way back. Should he have included this contingency in his list of things that could go wrong? What action could he have taken to either prevent or correct it? This is not the time to find fault. This is the time to reinforce the importance of preplanning/contingency planning.

Even if you have to walk them through this process by continuously asking questions, it is essential that the employee leave the follow-up session with at least one lesson learned. The bottom line is that at this stage, you, as the coach, can only accept one of two things… either success or a lesson learned.

Third: Decide what to do next

Regardless of the outcome, you now must ask one simple question: "What are you going to do next time to (either):

1)   Make sure you are successful again?

2)   Make sure you don't make the same mistake again?

As in the last few steps, the key is to let the employee who is being coached do the talking. Buy-in occurs only when he consciously makes the decision and voices aloud what actions he is going to take. As a coach, you can't tell the employee what to do; he has to do this for himself. If the employee was successful, all that is needed is for the person to simply state he or she will continue the process. However, if the employee was unsuccessful, he or she needs to acknowledge that he or she will incorporate the "lessons learned" from the second part of this step of the process. Again, the value of this step is that the employee consciously accepts responsibility for either continuing his successful activities or correcting his own problem.

It doesn't take long to do it right!

Coaching for Buy-in and Results isn't a time-consuming activity. In the rush of a normal day some people might look at this process and believe they won't have time to learn and use it. The truth is, however, that even in the early stages of learning the process and becoming comfortable with its structure, it only takes a few extra minutes to implement.

It is more a question of effort and willingness to use the process than a question of extra time. It may be a trite statement, but if we can find time to fix something after we do it wrong, then we can certainly find the extra time to do the job right the first time. It's a matter of desire and willingness, not a question of available time. This isn't meant to be a formal half-hour discussion; it is a tool to enhance the effectiveness of your communication. Once you and your employees get the hang of it, you can go through the first four steps of the process in less than ten minutes for most situations and you will normally get through the fifth step in less than five minutes. (You will need to allocate approximately 10 to 30 minutes for planning prior to each coaching session; more time at first, then progressively less as you become proficient.)

The beauty of this technique is that, as you become proficient as a coach, you may actually spend less time communicating than before you started using this process and you will get far better results.

Most importantly, you can now shift performance responsibility squarely onto the shoulders of the person being coached. With the employee's acceptance of responsibility, the coach's available time to manage and direct the team is expanded exponentially based on the number of employees being coached. Additionally, this creates a true sense of unity within the workgroup. The final benefit is that your employees will have the satisfaction of knowing they are being listened to, are being given the opportunity to participate in the process and the chance to accept responsibility for their actions or inactions.

The bottom line is that the follow-up and follow through process works. It is the glue that holds the entire coaching process together by ensuring the employee accepts responsibility for delivering the desired results and receives appropriate credit when they succeed. With the exception of outright refusal, it works every time!

There is no argument that, in the beginning, it may take extra time and effort to use this process. But the question isn't how much extra time and effort is required versus simply giving an order or directive. The question is: do you want to get results and eliminate excuses?

Chapter Summary

Key points included in this chapter included:

- Mastering the coaching process takes time for both the coach and the employee to become effective and comfortable with it.

- This step is essential to the success of the process: What you don't measure you can't manage.

- This step has three distinct parts that need to be followed in sequence:

    One - Review the results—obtain a factual statement of whether the agreed-on goal, as defined in step one, was achieved. Yes or No. If yes, at what level: minimal, primary or visionary?

    Two - Determine if the employee succeeded or learned something -- this requires a factual review of the results; "No Excuses."

    Three - Decide what you will do next -- will your employee continue to use the same approach or will he make an adjustment based on the lessons learned?

- Once the coach and employee become familiar with the process, the first four steps should take less than ten minutes, in most cases. The fifth step is typically accomplished in less than five minutes. (An additional 10 to 30 minutes should be allocated for planning before every Coaching session.)

Notes

Chapter X

What If It Doesn't Work?

> *"Those not fired with enthusiasm will be fired with enthusiasm."*
>
> *Vince Lombardi*

> *"Teach - Tolerate - Terminate."*
>
> *Joy Sheldon*

At the beginning, I stated this process would work with any but the most recalcitrant employee. But what do you do with an employee who simply refuses to participate and accept responsibility for himself and his work?

Use this process to obtain change. Just as it can be used for routine work assignments and responsibilities it can also be used for "attitude adjustments" and behavioral changes. In step one, you have to be very clear about the behaviors and the performance level you expect. But stating what you want is not enough; you must also clearly state what

125

behaviors and performance levels will not be tolerated and the employee must be very clear in restating his understanding of the acceptable behaviors and/or performance levels. It is essential that you speak in concrete terms and that the employee not be allowed to respond with generalities.

Being specific is the key to success. Take the time to ensure you know, in the simplest terms, exactly what you expect and how you can differentiate success from failure. The responsibility for success at this stage rests solely on the coach.

In Step 2: "Tell 'em "Why"... Not "How," what's in it for them is -- bottom line -- their job and future employment. This is not the time to pull any punches. If you've tried coaching for job performance and failed, or if you've put the employee on notice for failure to perform, there can be no question that it's now time to draw the proverbial line in the sand. Follow through with steps three through five and then it's up to the employee to either change for the better or face the consequences that have been clearly spelled out.

And if the employee still hasn't met your expectations? *Fire him!*

Some managers view having to fire someone as a sign of weakness as well as a sign of failure on the part of the supervisor or manager responsible for firing the employee. However, in a "No Excuses" culture you're only hurting the rest of the team and sending out contradictory messages.

In "Fired Anyone Lately," *Sales & Marketing Management*, January 1996, Barry J. Farber, president of Farber Training Systems, Inc. writes:

"There are three basic reasons for firing salespeople *(and I would hasten to add that these reasons apply to virtually every employee, regardless of their position or job function):*

1)   They blatantly violate company policy or do something illegal or dangerous;

2)   Even after coaching, warnings and probation, they aren't exerting the effort that your company demands; or

3)   They just aren't made for selling *(or don't have the technical competence to perform their assigned duties regardless of their specific job assignment).*

Farber notes that firing someone isn't easy -- most managers are, by nature, optimists. But, he says, consider the consequences to the employee, the team and yourself if you fail to make a tough call. He

127

illustrates his point with a story about a sales representative he had to fire -- even though he liked him -- for lack of performance. Years later he ran into someone who had seen the former employee. According to him, the ex-employee was happy... he knew the sales manager had made the right decision.

I don't like firing people, but I've yet to see the time when, after giving the employee every opportunity to improve, that the whole team's morale didn't improve when that person was let go. More importantly, your employees will know you can be trusted because you have the ability to make tough decisions. Now you can spend more time with those who are trying to improve and get the job done. This is only fair to the rest of your team!

The payback for improving your good people will always be higher than your efforts to improve weak employees and will be infinitely higher than your efforts to improve those employees who do not want to improve.

Chapter Summary

Key points in this chapter included:

- The coaching process is an effective tool for use with employees who demonstrate attitude and behavior related performance problems.

- The key to successfully coaching behavioral changes is clear, precise, communications. The responsibility lies with the coach to be explicit in identifying the specific behavior characteristics and performance levels or behaviors that will not be tolerated.

- It is absolutely essential that the employee be able to clearly restate what is expected and what will no longer be tolerated. This is the only way the coach will be able to be sure the employee being coached understands what is expected of him.
- If these coaching efforts fail to deliver satisfactory results, the coach is left with only one option... fire the employee.

- Firing employees who refuse to meet, or cannot meet the accepted standards for performance and behavior is the only "fair" thing to do in respect to those employees who demonstrate acceptable behavioral performance.

Notes

Epilogue

What Is "Coaching For Buy-In And Results?"

What distinguishes a truly great leader/manager from a run-of-the-mill executive, manager or supervisor? It's his ability to get his employees to willingly take responsibility for their own performance... **the ability to get their work done to reach their goals and objectives through others**.

But that's only part of it. What distinguishes the truly great leaders from the run-of-the-mill managers is **their ability to consistently get extraordinary results from ordinary people.**

"Coaching For Buy-In and Results" is a technique, a process, that helps you, as the executive, manager or supervisor, do the job right and create a team that excels at delivering superior performance. It is a process that allows employees to accept responsibility for their own actions. It is the vehicle that allows employees to contribute to the solution, thus building their self-esteem, making them more valuable, and creating a sense of loyalty to the company... because they are *part of the team.*

It is a process that, when used properly and consistently, allows ordinary employees, regardless of their classification -- unskilled laborer, skilled craftsman, technician, sales person or professional, to consistently deliver extraordinary results!

This process is also the vehicle for creating real leaders. In sales, as in many other fields, it is common to see companies promote their best salesmen to the sales manager positions. Frankly, this is like taking your best aircraft mechanic and making him your pilot. They may share some common skills and capabilities, but without specific training for the new position, it is a recipe for disaster.

Just as we wouldn't expect the mechanic to know all the intricacies of knowing how to take off, navigate and land, we shouldn't expect our top performing employees to successfully transition into supervisory or management positions without the tools needed to ensure success. Creating a "No Excuses" culture and using the process of "Coaching for buy-in and results" are the tools needed to successfully transition into supervisory, management or executive positions, and accept the responsibilities of leadership.

Notes

Bibliography

Berglas, Steven, "When Money Talks, People Walk." *Inc.*, May 1996.

Bleech, James M. and Mutchler, David G., *Let's get results, not excuses!* Grand Rapids, MI, MBP Press, 1994.

Brewer, Geoffrey, "Seven Secrets to Building Employee Loyalty When You Can't Promise Job Security." *Performance*, December 1995.

Brewer, Geoffey, "Mind Reading: What drives top salespeople to greatness?" *Sales & Marketing Management*, May 1994.

Cohen, Andy, "Lighting a Fire Under Average Performers." *Sales & Marketing Management*, January 1996.

Covey, Stephen R., *The 7 Habits of Highly Effective People*, Stephen R. Covey, 1989.

Farber, Barry J., "Start at the Beginning." *Sales & Marketing Management*, March 1996.

Farber, Barry J., "Fired Anyone Lately?" *Sales & Marketing Management*, January 1996.

Farber, Barry J., "Be a Field Coach." *Sales & Marketing Management*, January 1995.

Hendricks, Mark, "Step By Step, Getting better all the time: the Japanese way of continuous improvement." *Entrepreneur*, March 1996.

"How to Build Relationships." *Sales & Marketing Management*, May 1996.

Kaczman, James, "Just fix it, your sales process, that is." *Sales & Marketing Management*, September 1995.

Nichols, Ralph G. and Stevens, Leonard A., "The busy executive spends 80% of his time listening to people... and still doesn't hear half of what is said." *Harvard Business Review*, September-October 1957.

Plumb, J. Charles "Courage, Choices and Challenges; Making Tough Choices in Challenging Times."

Motivational Presentation.   (805) 683-1969 telephone (805) 683-4142 fax.

"Person-to-Person: How to Give (And Receive) Feedback." *Sales & Marketing Management*, May 1996.

Quick, Thomas L., "When Your Salespeople Want to Move Ahead." *Sales & Marketing Management*, November 1990.

Royal, Weld F., "Pleading Their Case." *Sales & Marketing Management,* February 1995.

For additional information please contact:

Business Development Specialists, Inc.
5111-6 Baymeadows Road
Suite 222
Jacksonville, FL 32217-4899

Phone: (904) 730-0654
(800) 635-0654

Fax: (904) 737-3665

e-mail: cork@bdspec.com

Visit our Web Site: www.bdspec.com